P9-CJJ-498

THE TROLL OF SORA

Leslie Elizabeth Watts

TORONTO
OXFORD UNIVERSITY PRESS
1989

To Tony and Emily and Vincenzo,
the real Troll of Sora.

Once upon a time in a small village in Italy, there lived a woman and her daughter, Fragolina. Life could have been very pleasant for them except for just one thing: Fragolina was not happy with herself.

She was neither fat nor thin. She wasn't tall and she wasn't short. She wasn't plain, nor was she beautiful. She wasn't very young, but she wasn't very old either.

"How could anybody like someone who is so much in the middle?" she would ask herself. "Everyone must laugh at me when my back is turned."

Once this idea became stuck in her head, it grew and grew until Fragolina could think of nothing else. Whenever her friends came to call, she would bolt the door and shout, "I won't come out! Just leave me alone!"

After a while, of course, that is just what they did, and soon there was no one left to like Fragolina for herself because she wouldn't let anyone near her.

Naturally, Fragolina felt very much alone, and in her loneliness she began to eat—more and more.

4

It started with her favourite sweets, and then spread to breakfast, lunch, and dinner. The meals grew in size until they were so big that just one of them could have fed the entire village.

Fragolina's mother was in despair. No longer was her daughter in the middle. She was utterly huge.

Whenever Fragolina's mother went shopping in the market, which by now was two or three times a day, someone would be sure to snicker and ask, "How is your Fragolina today? Lovely as ever?"

Then everyone would start to laugh, and the poor woman's ears would turn red, though she tried to pretend not to hear.

As for Fragolina, whenever she went for a walk and met someone coming the other way, she would have to back up all the way to her gate because no one could pass her in the narrow streets of the village. So usually she just stayed at home and looked out the window.

One day when her mother returned from the market with ears as red as cranberries, Fragolina threw herself against her and wailed, "Mother, everyone has been laughing at me! Whatever shall I do? If only I were right in the middle again!"

Her mother made a clucking sound with her tongue and said, "If you spent less time worrying about the way you look and more time being happy with yourself you'd have no trouble."

But Fragolina continued to weep until her tears dribbled down the mountains of her cheeks and got lost somewhere among her three chins.

Her mother shook her head and sighed. "There's only one thing to do," she said. "In the market I've heard talk of the Troll of Sora. They say that although he is ugly, he is kind. He can do anything you ask if your heart is true. If this is so, then maybe he can put you back to being in the middle. Would you be happy then?"

Fragolina sniffled and wiped her eyes. "Oh, yes," she said. "Let's see if he can help."

They decided to write a letter at once, asking the troll to come and help them. And when her mother suggested that she begin that very evening to cut down on her eating, Fragolina decided not to have her usual bedtime snack of a whole apple pie with mozzarella cheese melted on top.

On the day that the troll arrived, Fragolina was sitting at the window waiting. She watched him open the gate, walk through, and close it carefully behind him. Then he took off his pointed cap, folded it over the crook of his arm, and rapped on the door with his wooden walking stick. Fragolina's mother answered the door and led the troll into the house.

His face was as wrinkled as a raisin, and he had small round ears with tufts of white hair sprouting from them. He was quite short and so stooped that his shoulders were as high as the tips of his ears.

Fragolina's mother showed him into the room and said, "This is my daughter. Do you think you can help?"

The troll passed his stick back and forth and looked straight into Fragolina's eyes. He looked so long and hard that Fragolina began to imagine that he could see what she was thinking.

"Well now, my dear," the troll said softly, "I can't imagine why you should be so unhappy. But since I can see that you are, I could give you something that would cure your troubles once and for all." He scratched his chin where a few white whiskers were growing and from his pocket he drew a large vial of clear, red liquid.

Fragolina's eyes shone with excitement as she began to reach for the vial, but the troll continued. "There will be a fee, of course."

"Of course," murmured Fragolina's mother as she reached for her purse.

"What's the fee?" Fragolina asked suspiciously, for she felt there was something hidden in the troll's wise old eyes.

The troll smiled. "Once you have become happy," he said, "you must give me your hand in marriage."

"What?" Fragolina cried rudely.

"Couldn't we just pay you with money?" her mother asked.

"I'm afraid not," said the troll. "It's the only way I will make my magic work. You see, I'm lonely living by myself. No one cares much for me the way I am. People see only an ugly old troll when they look at me. It's time I found a wife. That is my fee. Take it or leave it."

10

Fragolina's mother shook her head. "It's not exactly what we had in mind," she began.

But Fragolina stood up suddenly and held her hand out to the troll. "Very well," she said brightly. "If that is your price, I accept."

Fragolina's mother was very surprised, but knowing that her daughter was old enough to make her own decisions, she remained silent.

As the troll shook Fragolina's hand, she saw that his eyes were kind as well as wise, and she looked quickly away.

"Drink this potion," the troll said, handing her the vial. "One teaspoonful every morning, and whatever it is you wish for to make you happy will be yours. I will return in three months to take you to my home in Sora. Don't forget your promise, for once you have drunk the potion the magic is . . ."

"Oh, I won't forget," Fragolina interrupted with a little laugh.

And so the troll tapped his cane along the path to the front gate and all along the road back to Sora.

When he was well out of sight, Fragolina's mother turned to her daughter and said, "I hope that you have made the right decision."

But Fragolina began to giggle and dance around the room so heavily that her mother was sure she would go through the floor. "Don't worry about me, Mother," Fragolina sang as she spun around in circles. "I'm feeling happier already."

But as soon as her mother had left the room, Fragolina said to herself, "That troll is too old and ugly for me. There's no way he can force me to marry him. Besides, if the potion really works, why should I wish simply to be back in the middle again? Why shouldn't I wish to be tall and slender and young and beautiful? Then I would have all the friends I want and find a husband who deserves me."

Every morning Fragolina would get out of bed, put on her clothes, drink a spoonful of the red liquid, and wish with all her might to be tall and slender and young and beautiful. Then she would sit down to breakfast. But strangely enough she would find that her appetite had vanished. After one boiled egg and a glass of juice she would feel so full that she could hardly get out of her chair.

Lunch and dinner were much the same. And once, when her mother offered her a dish of ice cream for a bedtime snack, Fragolina said, "Mother, can't you see I've already eaten enough today to feed the entire village?"

As you can imagine, Fragolina soon began to lose weight. By the end of the first month she would walk down the village streets and people could pass her without too much difficulty. After six weeks her mother had to make her three new dresses because her old ones were so big that she tripped and fell when she put them on. People began to notice the change in her and no longer teased her mother, who had to go to the market only once a week by now.

But her mother began to suspect that there was more to this than Fragolina let on. For as each day passed, her daughter seemed to become not only more dainty, but also taller, younger, and far more beautiful.

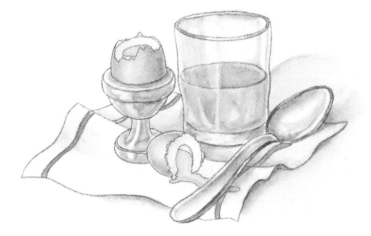

After two months had passed, Fragolina was the most beautiful girl in the village, and young men began to turn their heads as she walked by. Even that didn't make her happy. Fragolina ignored them all for suddenly they didn't seem good enough for her.

One day, only three weeks before the troll was due to return, Fragolina was hanging laundry in the front yard when a young count from a nearby village rode by on a dappled grey horse. He was very handsome, and from his clothes and fine steed, Fragolina decided that he must also be very rich. She smiled so sweetly that the count stopped to talk to her.

Fragolina's mother, who had been watching from the window, called her into the house. "Don't forget," she said sternly, "that the Troll of Sora is returning in just three weeks and that you have promised to marry him."

"Don't be silly, Mother," said Fragolina. "The count has only stopped to ask for directions." And she went back out to the yard to talk a little longer.

But in spite of what Fragolina had told her mother, the count returned every day for a week and a half, and it seemed to him that each time he saw Fragolina she was even lovelier than she had been the day before. In no time at all he was desperate to marry her. She was the only girl he had ever met who he felt was beautiful enough to be his wife. Fragolina, of course, agreed.

"You are a foolish girl!" scolded Fragolina's mother when she found out what her daughter was planning to do. "He only wants to marry you because he thinks you are beautiful. Do you suppose for one moment that he would have looked twice at you before you were so pretty? He doesn't love you for yourself. Oh, why couldn't you have just been satisfied with being in the middle? You would be better off with the troll whom you have already promised to marry. At least he is kind and wants you to be happy."

"Pooh!" scoffed Fragolina. "That ugly old troll doesn't deserve someone like me. Why, every young man in this village wishes that he could be my husband. I am the envy of every woman who sees me. And now I shall be a countess and have everything I want. Already I have this ruby ring. And just look at these pearls in my ears!"

Fragolina's mother shook her head and sighed. "Rubies are not friends and pearls will not bring you lasting happiness," she said sadly.

Nevertheless, Fragolina and the count set the date. The count wanted to be married as soon as possible, so Fragolina agreed to the following Saturday.

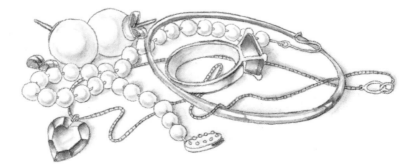

On the wedding day, Fragolina put on her white lace dress and fixed the matching veil over her shining hair. Just as she was admiring herself in the mirror, there was a knock on the front door. Thinking that the count's coach had arrived to take her to the church, Fragolina ran to the door and flung it open.

And there stood the Troll of Sora.

''Fragolina,'' he whispered as tears filled his round, green eyes. ''You've been waiting for me.'' And he knelt before her to kiss her hand.

But as his lips touched her fingers, Fragolina pulled away and gave him a hard shove. The troll tumbled backwards down the steps.

"Get away from here!" she shrieked. "Someone might see you!"

The troll stood up and rubbed his head. "I don't understand," he said. "You promised to marry me and I have come to take you to Sora. You are already wearing your bridal gown. Surely you have not forgotten?"

"Why would someone as beautiful as I marry an ugly old troll like you?" Fragolina hissed in a sour voice. "I am to marry a count on this very day, a man so rich and handsome that your eyes would bulge with envy if you saw him. I'll live in a fine house and have everything I want for the rest of my life. Now leave me at once before I call for help."

The troll gritted his teeth and smacked his walking stick against the palm of his hand. "Fragolina," he said, "I gave you the potion only because you were so unhappy. The truth is, you were far more lovely as you were than you are at this very moment. Marry your count if you must, but I feel sorry for what lies ahead. The magic will not last if you break your promise, and you will see, sooner than you think, that the count's heart is as empty as yours. He does not love you for yourself, only for your beauty."

"Words!" cried Fragolina. "Your words mean nothing to me. Now get out of my sight!"

The troll shook his head sadly, and once again he left Fragolina's house, tapping his cane as he went. Fragolina pulled her veil down over her frowning face and waited with her mother for the coach to come.

The church was filled with people. The organ played loudly as the bride started down the aisle. But, with each step she took, Fragolina became more nervous. The troll's words still rang in her ears, and she began to fear that she did not really love the handsome count and that he did not love her. By the time she had reached the altar, he seemed like a stranger to her.

There was a glint of gold as the count brought the wedding band from his vest pocket. Suddenly Fragolina was filled with terrible regret.

"Oh, I wish I'd been satisfied when I was in the middle," she thought. "I wish there had never been any magic at all. And I wish I had married the Troll of Sora who liked me as I was."

No sooner had she made the third wish than a sudden breeze blew through the church and lifted the veil from Fragolina's face. To the count's utter surprise, the person underneath was no longer the most beautiful girl in the village, but someone completely different. Someone who was right in the middle.

Just as the troll had known he would, the count stepped back
and gasped, "I can't marry you! You are not beautiful enough to
be my countess. You don't deserve a man like me!"

"You're right!" shouted Fragolina as she ran out of the church.
"I deserve to find someone who loves me for who I am, not for
how I look." With that the count fainted dead away, and Fragolina
ran from sight down the road with her mother close behind.

By the time she caught up with the troll, he was almost home.
She told him how sorry she was and that she finally understood

what he and her mother had been trying to tell her. Then she asked him so nicely if he would still marry her that he couldn't possibly stay angry.

"Will you be happy and love me as I am?" he asked.

"Yes," she promised.

The troll looked long and hard into Fragolina's eyes, and then he smiled, for he saw that at last her heart was true. They were wed that same afternoon with Fragolina's mother as their only guest.

Fragolina and the troll lived happily together for many years and had seven children. One was fat, one was slender, one was short, one was tall, one was plain, one was beautiful, and one was somewhere in the middle. But all of them were happy just the way they were—even the one whose face was as wrinkled as a raisin.

Oxford University Press, 70 Wynford Drive, Don Mills, Ontario, M3C 1J9

Toronto Oxford New York Delhi Bombay Calcutta Madras Karachi
Petaling Jaya Singapore Hong Kong Tokyo Nairobi Dar es Salaam
Cape Town Melbourne Auckland
and associated companies in
Berlin Ibadan

Canadian Cataloguing in Publication Data

Watts, Leslie Elizabeth, 1961—
The troll of Sora

ISBN 0-19-540717-2

I. Title.

PS8595.A88T76 1989   jC813'.54   C89-090075-2
PR9199.3.W37Tr 1989

Text and illustrations © Leslie Elizabeth Watts 1989
Oxford is a trademark of Oxford University Press
1 2 3 4 — 2 1 0 9
Printed in Hong Kong